Do You Know about Amphibians?

Buffy Silverman

Lerner Publications Company
Minneapolis

Remembering Ben
-B.S.

Lerner Publications Company
A division of Lerner Publishing Group, Inc.
241 First Avenue North
Minneapolis, MN 55401 U.S.A.

Website address: www.lernerbooks.com

Library of Congress Cataloging-in-Publication Data

Silverman, Buffy.
    Do you know about Amphibians? / by Buffy Silverman.
        p.   cm. — (Lightning bolt books™ — Meet the animal groups)
    Includes index.
    ISBN 978–0–8225–7543–6 (lib. bdg. : alk. paper)
    1. Amphibians—Juvenile literature. I. Title.
    QL644.2.S55 2010
    597.8—dc22   2007030540

Manufactured in the United States of America
1 2 3 4 5 6 — BP — 15 14 13 12 11 10

Contents

What Is an Amphibian?

Tadpoles swim in a pond. They wiggle their tails from side to side.

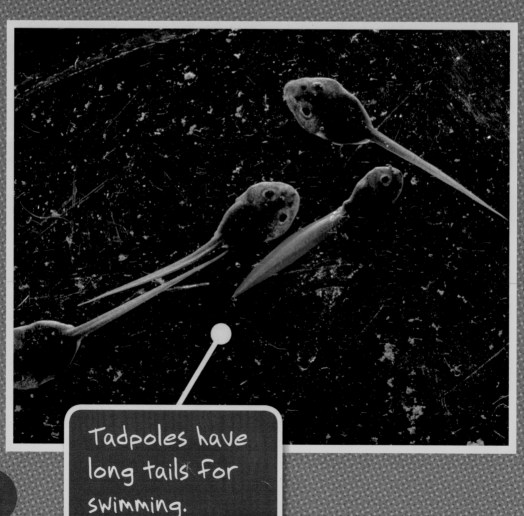

Tadpoles have long tails for swimming.

Tadpoles change as they grow.

What do they become?

Tadpoles grow legs.

Frogs! They leap out of water and hop across land. Frogs are amphibians. Toads and salamanders are amphibians too.

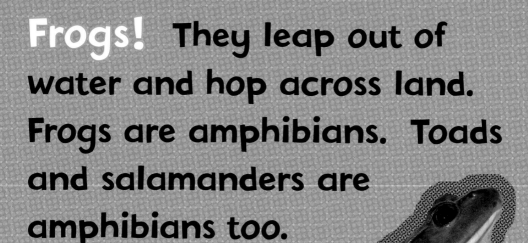

A frog's long back legs help it leap on land and swim in water.

Most young amphibians start their lives in water. Most adults live on land.

All amphibians have backbones. You can see this frog's backbone under its smooth skin.

Amphibians cannot make their own body heat. Their bodies get cold when the air is cold. They get warmer when the air is warm. They are ectotherms.

Two frogs warm up on a sunny log.

Many amphibians live where it is always warm. This spadefoot toad lives in the hot desert. It stays cool by burying itself underground.

Amphibians Lay Eggs

Spotted salamanders crawl in a forest on a rainy spring night.

Some spotted salamanders have yellow spots.

They find a pond. There they lay a clump of eggs. The eggs do not have shells. They are covered in a jelly.

A spotted salamander rests near its eggs.

Toads also lay eggs. They lay them in long strings.

Inside each egg, a tadpole grows.

These are toad eggs. One toad can lay thousands of eggs at a time.

Soon tadpoles hatch from the eggs. The tadpoles eat tiny water plants.

Groups of tadpoles stay together and eat.

This bird caught a tadpole.

Tadpoles swim together to stay safe. Fish, birds, snakes, turtles, and insects all eat tadpoles.

Male poison dart frogs guard their eggs. Tiny tadpoles hatch from the eggs. They wiggle onto their dad's back. He carries them to water.

A male poison dart frog carries two tadpoles to water.

This bullfrog tadpole has grown legs.

Amphibians Grow and Change

An amphibian's body shape changes as it grows. The tiny tadpole hatches from an egg and grows quickly. Its back legs grow first. Then tiny front legs appear. Its tail disappears. This change is called metamorphosis.

The tadpole changes in other ways too. Soon it will eat insects instead of water plants. It grows a long, sticky tongue to catch flies.

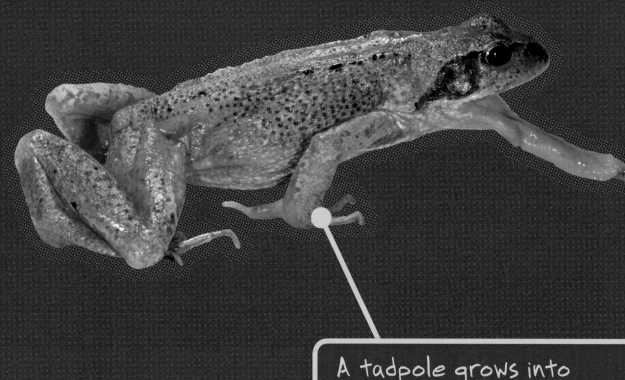

A tadpole grows into a frog. It uses its tongue to catch a bug.

The tadpole grows eardrums.
What will it hear?
Frog songs! Male frogs call to
females in the spring.

Can you see this frog's eardrum?

Young amphibians breathe underwater with gills. This young spotted salamander has feathery gills.

Soon the salamander's legs grow longer. The fin along its tail shrinks. Its gills disappear. Lungs grow. Then it breathes air with its lungs.

This adult spotted salamander used to have gills. Now it has lungs and breathes air.

A tiger salamander also breathes through its damp skin. It digs holes underground. The wet ground keeps its skin damp.

Some amphibians always live underwater. Adult mud puppies swim in lakes and streams. They keep their bushy gills.

An adult mud puppy catches a crayfish underwater.

Amphibians Stay Safe

Some amphibians stay safe by hiding below ground. Marbled salamanders creep beneath logs. They hide there from enemies.

Some amphibians blend in.
Camouflage helps them stay safe.
Can you spot the gray tree frog?

The bright color of a golden poison frog warns hunters to stay away. The frog's poison makes animals sick.

Stay away from this golden poison frog!

How does the wood frog live in the cold winter? It hibernates. Water inside its body turns to ice. The ice melts in the spring.

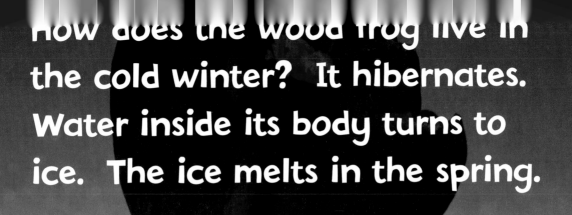

A wood frog hides in the soil in winter. It comes out of hibernation in the spring.

Then the frog hops away.

Fun Facts

Legless Wonders

Amphibians called caecilians have no legs. Caecilians look like worms. Their tiny eyes can see only light and dark.

Sky-High Tadpoles

Some poison arrow frogs carry tadpoles high into a tree. The father frog drops a tadpole in its own tiny pool of water in a tree trunk. The tadpole stays there until it changes into a frog.

Giant Salamanders

Japanese giant salamanders can grow longer than you! They grow for their entire lives.

Who Is the Parent?

Match the young amphibian with its parent.

Parent	Young

A

1

B

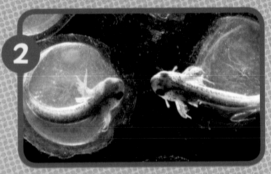

2

C

3

Check your answers on page 31

Glossary

amphibian: an animal with smooth skin that usually lives part of its life in water and part of its life on land. Frogs, toads, salamanders, and caecilians are amphibians.

camouflage: coloring that helps an animal blend in with the things around it

ectotherm: an animal whose body temperature changes when the temperature of its surroundings changes

eardrum: the part of the ear that vibrates to sound

gill: a part of the body that some animals use for breathing underwater

hibernates: spends the winter in a sleeplike state. When animals hibernate, they have a lower body temperature, breathe less often, and use little energy.

lung: a body part that some animals use to breathe air

metamorphosis: changes in the form of some animals as they grow

tadpole: a young frog or toad that has hatched from an egg

Further Reading

All about Frogs for Kids and Teachers
http://www.kiddyhouse.com/Themes/frogs
Learn about record-breaking frogs, where frogs live, what they eat, and more.

Amphibians
http://animals.nationalgeographic.com/animals/amphibians.html
Learn all about amphibians' lives in water and on land.

Bishop, Nic. *Nic Bishop Frogs.* New York: Scholastic, 2008.

Bredeson, Carmen. *Fun Facts about Salamanders.* Berkeley Heights, NJ: Enslow Publishers, 2008.

Know Your Frogs
http://www.dnr.state.wi.us/org/caer/ce/eek/critter/amphibian/frogident.htm
Learn to identify many different kinds of frogs and hear their songs.

Pyers, Greg. *Why Am I an Amphibian?* Chicago: Raintree, 2006.

Answer key for page 29:
A is a bullfrog. It is the parent of 3.
B is a mud puppy. It is the parent of 1.
C is a spotted salamander. It is the parent of 2.

index

Photo Acknowledgments

The images in this book are used with the permission of: © iStockphoto.com/Kevin Snair,
p. 1; © Corel Professional Photos, p. 2; © iStockphoto.com/Juli Van Breemen, p. 4;
© Dorling Kindersley/Getty Images, p. 5; © American Images, Inc/Stone/Getty Images,
p. 6; © BIOS Gunther Michel/Peter Arnold, Inc., p. 7; © iStockphoto.com/Jozsef Szasz-
Fabian, p. 8; © A. Noellert/Peter Arnold, Inc., p. 9; © Scott Camazine/Alamy, p. 10;
© Gustov W. Verderber/Visuals Unlimited, Inc., p. 11; © Gary Meszaros/Visuals Unlimited,
Inc., pp. 12, 16, 21, 23, 29 (center left and bottom left); © Hans Pfletschinger/Peter Arnold,
Inc., p. 13; © Steve Maslowski/Visuals Unlimited, Inc., p. 14; © Michael & Patricia Fogdon/
Minden Pictures, p. 15; © Kim Taylor and Jane Burton/Dorling Kindersley/Getty Images,
p. 18; © Joe McDonald/Visuals Unlimited/Getty Images, p. 19; © Dwight Kuhn, pp. 20, 25,
29 (center right); © John Parke/Visuals Unlimited, Inc., p. 22; © Doug Wechsler/naturepl.
com, p. 24; © blickwinkel/Alamy, p. 26; © Kitchin & Hurst/leesonphoto.com, p. 27; © Gail
Shurnway/Photographers Choice RR/Getty Images, p. 28; © iStockphoto.com/Audrey
Roorda, p. 29 (top left); © R.D. Bartlett, p. 29 (top right); © iStockphoto.com/Ron Brancato,
p. 29 (bottom right); © iStockphoto.com/Bruce MacQueen, p. 30.

Front cover: © Pete Oxford/Minden Pictures (main); © Kamensky | Dreamstime.com (top
left); © Corbis/Royalty-free (center left); © Byron Jorjorian/Alamy (top right).